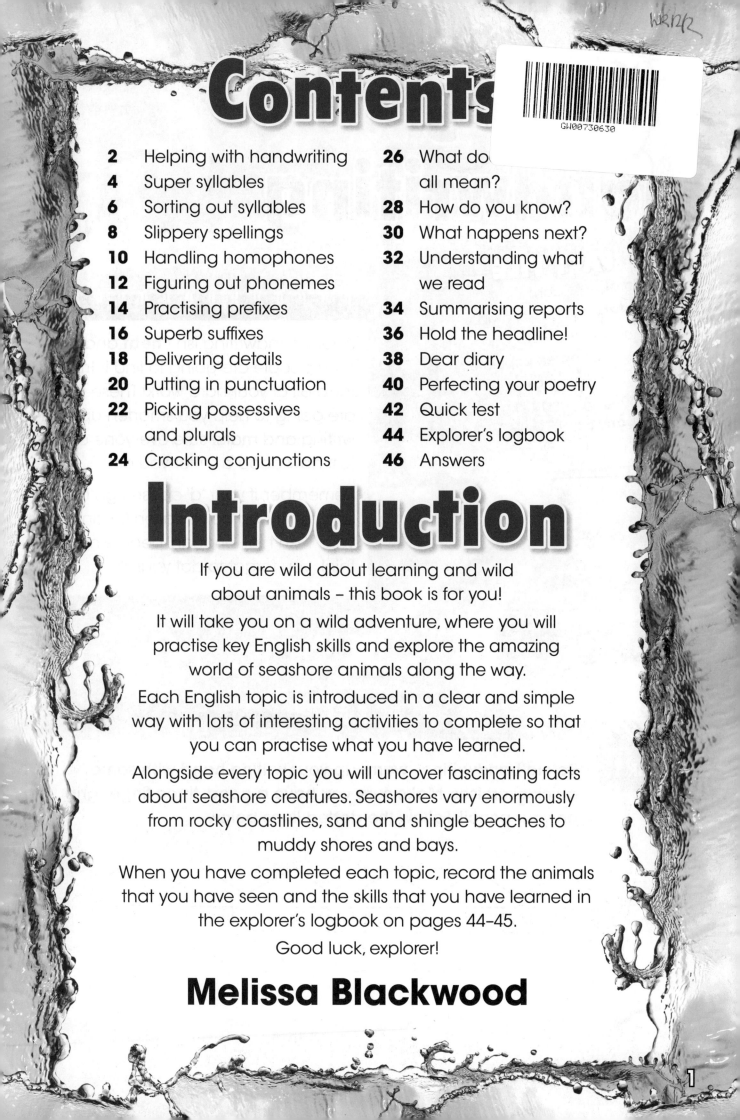

# Contents

# Introduction

If you are wild about learning and wild about animals – this book is for you!

It will take you on a wild adventure, where you will practise key English skills and explore the amazing world of seashore animals along the way.

Each English topic is introduced in a clear and simple way with lots of interesting activities to complete so that you can practise what you have learned.

Alongside every topic you will uncover fascinating facts about seashore creatures. Seashores vary enormously from rocky coastlines, sand and shingle beaches to muddy shores and bays.

When you have completed each topic, record the animals that you have seen and the skills that you have learned in the explorer's logbook on pages 44–45.

Good luck, explorer!

## Melissa Blackwood

# Helping with handwriting

## FACT FILE

**Animal:** Pelican

**Habitat:** Found worldwide, near water and densely populated fishing areas

**Weight:** Around 13 kg

**Lifespan:** 5 to 15 years

**Diet:** Fish

If your handwriting isn't **neat** and **tidy**, then people are going to find it tricky to read all of your hard work! These pages are going to help you smarten up your writing and make sure everyone can see just how good a writer you are.

Remember, if your 'd' doesn't go high enough it can be mistaken for an 'a'; if your 'l' isn't tall enough, people might think you forgot to dot your 'i'!

**Task 1**

Before handwriting, warm up your writing hand with some quick exercises. Make sure you have a good, three-finger grip on your pencil. Follow the dotted lines below.

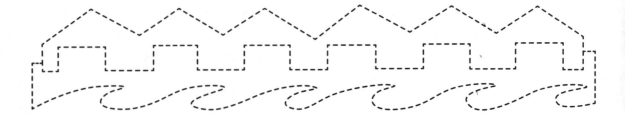

**Task 2**  Practice joining tall and short letters.

bm bm

di di

ch ch

rk rk

ln ln

st st

**WILD FACT**

The American white pelican can hold approximately 11.5 litres of water in its bill.

**Task 3**  Now you've mastered those, join letters that hang below the line.

fo fo

ng ng

ji ji

pa pa

qu qu

ly ly

**WILD FACT**

Young pelicans feed by sticking their bills into their parents' throats to retrieve food.

**Exploring Further ...**

Now you've practised with some letters, let's see what you can do with them. Rewrite this sentence on the lines below, using your **best handwriting**.

My handwriting is awesome!

**Now follow the line... to pages 44–45 to record what you have learned in your explorer's logbook.**

3

# Super syllables

A **syllable** is the single unit of sound used to make up a word or part of a word. A word with one syllable is called **monosyllabic**.

*sea, crab*

A word with two syllables is called **disyllabic**.

*limpet (lim-pet), rockpool (rock-pool)*

A word with three or more syllables is called **polysyllabic**.

*jellyfish (jell-y-fish), submarine (sub-ma-rine)*

An easy way to count how many syllables is to **clap** along with the word as you say it slowly.

## FACT FILE

| | |
|---|---|
| Animal: | Sea anemone |
| Habitat: | Coastal waters around the world |
| Size: | Up to 180 cm across |
| Diet: | Snails, slugs and small fish |

**Task 1** Count how many syllables are in these words and write the number in the box.

a earth ☐   b accident ☐

c circle ☐   d special ☐

e anemone ☐   f ocean ☐

g strength ☐   h peculiar ☐

i pressure ☐   j unidentified ☐

## WILD FACT

Anemones are cnidarians, meaning they can live indefinitely by reproducing themselves. In fact, a sea anemone cut into two or more pieces will eventually grow into two or more anemones!

**Task 2**  Add the missing syllables to complete each word.

a  _____ a _____          Definition: A musical keyboard.

b  _____ tory          Definition: The study of the past.

c  _____ en _____          Definition: Look at this to find out
                                                                        the day, month and year.

d  Ex _____ i _____          Definition: A scientific procedure.

**WILD FACT**

Some anemones fight other anemones by striking them with their tentacles!

**Task 3**  Think of a word for each definition.

a  Monosyllabic word _____
   Definition: Pump in the body that keeps blood circulating.

b  Disyllabic word _____
   Definition: A way to describe someone or something well-known.

c  Disyllabic word _____
   Definition: People always 'on the go' and bees are described as this.

d  Polysyllabic word _____
   Definition: The opposite of forget.

**Exploring Further ...**

Say what you see in each picture below, and count the syllables.
Join each picture to the correct rockpool.

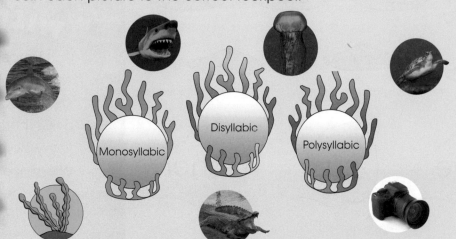

Monosyllabic    Disyllabic    Polysyllabic

**Now wave gently to pages 44–45 to record what you
have learned in your explorer's logbook.**

# Sorting out syllables

Some words are tricky to spell. The 'ure' sound (**phoneme**) at the end of words can be spelt **ture** or **sure** or **cher**.

Most words have the **ture** spelling.

*adventure, miniature*

Words sounding like they have a 'zh' sound have **sure**.

*measure, treasure*

Words that have a **ch** or **tch** at the end of the root end with **cher**.

*teacher, watcher*

## FACT FILE

| | |
|---|---|
| **Animal:** | Limpet |
| **Habitat:** | Shorelines throughout the world, from the UK to Australia |
| **Weight:** | 4 to 8 g |
| **Lifespan:** | 10 to 20 years |
| **Diet:** | Algae: the plants and seaweed found under the sea |

**Task 1**

Match the beginning and endings of the words by joining the limpets to the rocks.

 cat
 cap
 mea
 punc
 cul
 ri
 tea

 -ture
 -sure
 -cher

## WILD FACT

Limpets have a cone-shaped shell as this stronger shape helps them survive the heavy, stormy seas they often face throughout the year.

## WILD FACT

Limpets move around the rock to find food but always return to the same spot when they want to rest.

### Task 2

Sort the words below into the table according to the number of syllables that each has.

| Disyllabic words | Trisyllabic words | Polysyllabic words |
|---|---|---|
|  |  |  |
|  |  |  |
|  |  |  |
|  |  |  |
|  |  |  |

adventure      future      miniature

treasure      leisure      preacher      nature

enclosure      furniture      agriculture

### Task 3

Draw a limpet shell around the correct word to match the clue!

**Clue**

a  A broken bone:                     leisure       fracture       future

b  Where horses and cows are kept:   pasture       closure        rancher

c  Carry an injured person on this:    ranger        texture        stretcher

d  A way to measure how             agriculture    temperature    furniture
warm it is:

### Exploring Further ...

Use as many words as you can ending in **ture**, **sure** or **cher**, to write two silly sentences.

For example: The minia**ture** ar**cher** was in rap**ture** over the trea**sure**.

_____

_____

_____

**Now turn to pages 44–45 to record what you have learned in your explorer's logbook.**

# Slippery spellings

Correct **spellings** are very important. Some words **sound the same** but may be **spelt differently**. See if you can sort out the correct spellings from all the mistakes!

## FACT FILE

**Animal:** Jellyfish
**Habitat:** All of the world's oceans
**Weight:** Box jellyfish weigh around 2 kg
**Lifespan:** Most live less than one year
**Diet:** Plankton

| Task 1 | Choose the correct spelling in the jellyfish below to complete the fascinating facts. Write the correct word in the space. |

**a** There are almost 1500 _____ types of jellyfish in the world.

 diferent
 different
 difurent

**b** Jellyfish exposed to UV light _____ to glow!

 appear
 apear
 appier

**c** Jellyfish _____ through the skin on every part of their body.

 breeth
 breaf
 breathe

WILD FACT

A group of jellyfish is called a 'bloom', 'swarm' or 'smack'.

**Task 2**

Put a circle around the five spelling mistakes in this paragraph.

Many people find the appearance of the jellyfish strainge. Some jellyfish are almost invisible in water, as their see-throogh bodies make them very diffecult for swimmers to spot. To make things worse, jellyfish often arive in coastal areas without any warning, taking swimmers and fishermen by suprise.

**Task 3**

Look at the spelling mistakes you found in Task 2. Write the correct spellings of these words in the jellyfish.

1 _____
2 _____
3 _____
4 _____
5 _____

WILD FACT

Jellyfish don't have brains!

**Exploring Further ...**

Can you unscramble the tentacles and find out what some species of jellyfish are called?

*Hint: Unscrambled names: lion's mane, cross, box, man o'war*

**Now float to pages 44–45 to record what you have learned in your explorer's logbook.**

# Handling homophones

**WILD FACT**

Hermit crabs like a crowd and are often seen in groups of 100 or more on the beach.

**Homophones** are words which rather confusingly **sound the same** but have very **different meanings**. To make things even trickier, they can even have almost the same spelling.

*The crab went out to **see** . . . = The crab went to look at something.*

*The crab went out to **sea** . . . = The crab went for a swim.*

## FACT FILE

**Animal:** Hermit crab
**Habitat:** Ocean waters worldwide
**Weight:** From 200 mg to 4 g
**Lifespan:** A few months to 30 years
**Diet:** Small fish and invertebrates including worms

**Task 1** Match the crab to the shell that has the same-sounding word on it, even if the spelling and meaning are quite different.

fair
write
no
knew
here
knight

night
fare
hear
right
new
know

**Task 2**  Add the correct word to the sentence so that it makes sense.

**whole / hole**

**a** This doughnut has a _____ in the middle.

I can eat a _____ doughnut in one bite.

**night / knight**

**b** It gets dark at _____.

The _____ rides on a white horse.

**WILD FACT**

The shell of the hermit crab is not its own, but one that once belonged to another animal.

**Task 3**  Draw a line to match the word to the correct meaning.

grown          Our feet have five of each!

toe            To exchange something for money.

cell           A deep sound made to show pain or sadness.

groan          To pull along on the end of a rope or chain.

tow            To have become larger.

sell           A very small room in which a prisoner is put.

**Exploring Further ...**

To play this game you will need: tweezers, paper, a pen and another player!

Write each homophone from these two pages on its own piece of paper. Using the tweezers as 'crab claws', ask the other player to pick out the pairs of words that sound the same.

**Now scuttle to pages 44–45 to record what you have learned in your explorer's logbook.**

11

# Figuring out phonemes

On the following pages we are going to look at some different ways of writing the same **sound**. Sounds in words are called **phonemes**. When you learn to read, you often sound out the phonemes.

f-l-a-g = flag          l-i-f-t-s = lifts

Some sounds are represented by more than one letter.

'qu' and 'ir' in 'squirt', or 'ch' and 'air' in 'chair'

A **grapheme** is how the phoneme is written. Some phonemes can be written using different letters.

The phoneme 'ee' can be written 'ee' as in 'tree'; 'ea' as in 'beat', 'ie' as in 'chief' or 'ei' as in 'ceiling'

## FACT FILE

**Animal:** Sea squirt
**Habitat:** Warm, tropical waters
**Weight:** Up to 200 g
**Lifespan:** 7 to 30 years
**Diet:** They filter nutritious particles out of the water

**Task 1** Choose the correct phoneme from the choice given in brackets and complete the word.

a  ca _____ (**tch / ch**)

b  cli _____ (**m / mb**)

c  (**kn / nn**) _____ it

d  (**r / wr**) _____ ong

e  (**n / kn / gn**) _____ ear

f  pin _____ (**ch/tch**)

g  (**ch / c / ck**) _____ emist

h  (**f / ph / ff**) _____ one

i  (**n/ kn**) _____ owledge

j  le _____ (**j / dge**)

## Task 2

The following words have the wrong long vowel grapheme. Write the word with its correct grapheme.

| | | | |
|---|---|---|---|
| fr**oo**t | | w**ate** | |
| g**i**de | | wr**oa**t | |
| br**y**t | | compl**ea**t | |
| gr**oo**p | | br**ie**the | |
| b**e**de | | extr**ea**m | |

**WILD FACT**

Sea squirts can vary from just 3 cm to 30 cm in length, depending on the species and its habitat.

## Task 3

Circle the word whose phoneme is said differently.

a **ch**imp   s**ch**ool   **ch**eat   **ch**ill   su**ch**

b w**eigh**t   h**eigh**t   fr**eigh**t   n**eigh**bour   **eigh**teen

c peng**ui**n   g**ui**de   acq**ui**re   q**ui**et   inq**ui**re

d sw**a**llow   **a**rrive   c**a**lendar   **a**crobat   pl**a**nkton

e br**ea**th   s**ea**   ah**ea**d   d**ea**th   l**ea**ther

**WILD FACT**

Sea squirts are normally filter feeders, but some really large species of sea squirts, found in the deep ocean, are known to trap and ingest small animals, including fish and jellyfish.

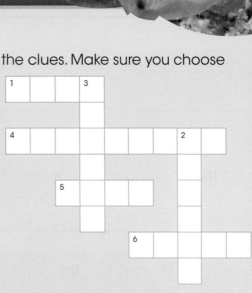

### Exploring Further ...

Complete the crossword using the clues. Make sure you choose the correct phoneme!

**Across**
1. Coral _____
4. Long tentacled sea creature
5. 12 months
6. Another word for Earth

**Down**
2. The animal featured on this page
3. Type of feeder a sea squirt is

**Now squirt to pages 44–45 to record what you have learned in your explorer's logbook.**

# Practising prefixes

A **prefix** can be a group of letters or a short word. Adding a prefix to the **start** of the word changes the meaning of the word.

legal ⟶ <u>il</u>legal

possible ⟶ <u>im</u>possible

regular ⟶ <u>ir</u>regular

expensive ⟶ <u>in</u>expensive

The prefixes **in**, **il**, **ir** and **im** change the meaning of the word to the **negative** or **opposite** meaning. Work through the tasks and discover the rules!

## FACT FILE

| | |
|---|---|
| **Animal:** | Albatross |
| **Habitat:** | The Pacific, southern Atlantic and Indian Oceans and into the Antarctic region |
| **Weight:** | Up to 10 kg |
| **Lifespan:** | Up to 50 years |
| **Diet:** | Mainly fish |

**Task 1** An albatross has found these words. Write them in the nests with the correct prefixes.

| | | | | |
|---|---|---|---|---|
| illicit | irregular | illuminate | indescribable | immature |
| impersonal | irreplaceable | informer | improbable | irrational |

**in**

**ir**

**im**

**il**

14

## Task 2

Look at the words in Task 1 again.
Match a red and a blue box to create a set of rules.

| | |
|---|---|
| Use **il** for words that | begin with 'l' |
| Use **ir** for words that | begin with 'm' or 'p' |
| Use **im** for words that | begin with all other letters |
| Use **in** for words that | begin with 'r' |

## Task 3

Now apply your rules to the following words to check they work.

| Root word | Add correct prefix |
|---|---|
| legal | |
| correct | |
| responsible | |
| formal | |
| expensive | |
| visible | |
| possible | |

**WILD FACT**

These flying giants have the longest wingspan of any bird – up to 3.5 metres.

**WILD FACT**

Some albatross species were heavily hunted for feathers that were used to decorate women's hats.

### Exploring Further ...

Starting at 'in', colour in a path across the maze to correctly join the prefixes and root words. What is the longest path you can make?

| in | active | im | legible | in | correct |
|---|---|---|---|---|---|
| il | migrant | possible | ir | polite | il |
| formal | in | il | legal | im | right |
| ir | im | expensive | ir | luminate | in |
| patient | correct | im | regular | il | relevant |
| responsible | il | in | patient | former | im |

**Now glide to pages 44–45 to record what you have learned in your explorer's logbook.**

# Superb suffixes

**WILD FACT**

The red sea urchin has the longest lifespan on Earth. It can survive up to 200 years in the wild!

A **suffix** is a group of letters added to the **end** of a word to change its meaning. We will look at the suffix **ous**. This changes a word into an **adjective**.

adventure ⟶ adventur<u>ous</u>

If the word ends in **ge**, keep the **e** and add **ous**.

outrage ⟶ outrag<u>eous</u>

If the word ends in **y**, change it to **i** and add **ous**.

fury ⟶ fur<u>ious</u>

**Task 1**  Change each word to an adjective by adding **ous**.

**a** melody  _____

**b** adventure  _____

**c** danger  _____

**d** glory  _____

**e** courage  _____

**f** fury  _____

**FACT FILE**

| | |
|---|---|
| **Animal:** | Sea urchin |
| **Habitat:** | All seawaters – warm or cold |
| **Weight:** | Up to 5.5 kg when fully grown |
| **Lifespan:** | Up to 30 years |
| **Diet:** | Seaweed, algae and plankton |

**WILD FACT**

Certain species of sea urchin have spikes filled with venom!

**Task 2** Change the root word in brackets to an adjective to complete the sentence.

a The sea urchin can be a _____ creature. (**danger**)

b The spines of the sea urchin may be _____. (**poison**)

c Sea urchins are not _____. (**nerve**)

d Sea urchins are not found in _____ regions. (**mountain**)

e Sea urchins are found in _____ sizes, depending on the water temperature of the ocean they live in. (**vary**)

**Task 3** These two words do not follow the rules given in the introduction. Can you explain the rules for adding the suffix **ous** to these words?

crustacean ⟶ crustaceous          amphibian ⟶ amphibious

_____

_____

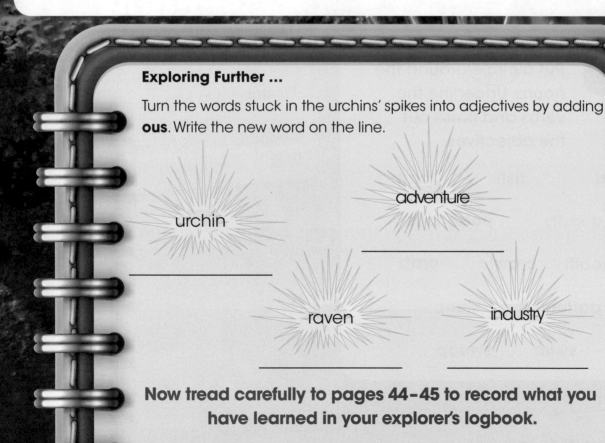

**Exploring Further ...**

Turn the words stuck in the urchins' spikes into adjectives by adding **ous**. Write the new word on the line.

adventure

urchin

_____

raven          industry

_____          _____

**Now tread carefully to pages 44–45 to record what you have learned in your explorer's logbook.**

# Delivering details

One of the easiest ways to make your writing more **interesting** to the reader is to add lots more **information** about the things you are mentioning. 'The dogfish . . .' may not sound all that interesting, but 'The poisonous, spiny dogfish . . .' may get your attention! This is **expanding** information about a noun by adding **adjectives** and is called an **expanded noun phrase**. You can also add detail at the beginning of the sentence by adding a short phrase called a **fronted adverbial**. It is followed by a comma, then the rest of the sentence.

*The dogfish swam away + fronted adverbial =*
*<u>Without warning</u>, the dogfish swam away.*

## FACT FILE

| | |
|---|---|
| **Animal:** | Dogfish |
| **Habitat:** | The coastlines of the Atlantic, Pacific and Indian Oceans |
| **Weight:** | 3 to 5 kg. The maximum recorded weight was 9.8 kg! |
| **Lifespan:** | 25 to 80 years |
| **Diet:** | Fish, squid and crustaceans |

**Task 1**  Put a (circle) around the nouns. <u>Underline</u> the verbs and ~~cross out~~ the adjectives.

bird          fish          man

deadly          poisonous

smooth     crawl          crab

patterned          sleep

swim          swoop

**Task 2**

Draw a line to join up the sentence sections that you think should go together.

**WILD FACT**

The spikes on the back of the spiny dogfish are mildly poisonous and are mainly used in defence.

Gently,                          I go swimming.

Once a week,                     he leapt forward.

Suddenly,                        I love to read.

On holiday,                      he lifted up the baby.

**Task 3**

Below are different sections of sentences. Colour sections in the same colour to make an interesting or funny sentence!

The small, hairy

The beautiful

The overgrown

The deadly

teacher

The large, vicious

tarantula

garden          lady          rattle snake

climbed the tree.

is highly poisonous.

was a disgrace.

sat at the desk.          sang beautifully.

**WILD FACT**

The spiny dogfish is one of the most abundant species of shark in the world. It is also commonly known as the spiked dogfish, the codshark and the thorndog.

**Exploring Further ...**

Write your own sentence about a dogfish. How would you describe it? Where is it? What is it doing? How is it doing it? Try to get as much detail into your sentence as you can.

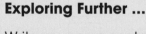

_____

_____

_____

**Now hunt your way to pages 44–45 to record what you have learned in your explorer's logbook.**

# Putting in punctuation

## FACT FILE

**Animal:** Sea slug
**Habitat:** Oceans throughout the world
**Weight:** Up to 14 kg
**Lifespan:** Generally a year or less
**Diet:** Plankton and decaying matter on the ocean floor

How you **punctuate** a sentence can change its **meaning**. For example:

*Private property? No! Swimming allowed.*

*Private property. No swimming allowed.*

Careful use of commas, faultless use of full stops and super use of speech marks are all important!

- Speech marks – "Hello."

- Exclamation mark – !

- Question mark – ?

- Full stop – .

- Comma – ,

- Capital letter – A

- Apostrophe – don't

---

**Task 1**  Add a **question mark** or an **exclamation mark** to each of the sentences.

a  It's amazing how much a sea slug eats ☐

b  Do sea slugs live on coral ☐

c  There are over 1000 species of sea slug ☐

d  How does a sea slug eat ☐

e  How many species of sea slug are there ☐

## WILD FACT

Some sea slugs are eaten by humans and have been used in traditional medicine in the Far East.

**Task 2**

Apostrophes can be used to show where a letter is missing. Choose a single word to replace the words in brackets. The first one has been done for you.

**WILD FACT**

The sea slug is also commonly referred to as a sea cucumber, mainly because of its shape and the fact that it lies so still it almost looks like an aquatic vegetable.

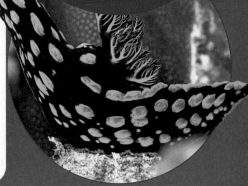

(**It is**) _It's_ the amazing sea slug! It may look like sea slugs (**do not**) _____ have teeth, but in fact they do – (**they are**) _____ just tiny. Some sea slugs are toxic, although they (**can not**) _____ hurt you with their spines as they (**are not**) _____ poisonous. In some countries, sea slugs are a delicacy! (**I have**) _____ never eaten sea slugs – have you?

**Task 3**  Correct these sentences and add punctuation marks.

**a**  more than 1000 species of sea slug live on australias great barrier reef

_____

_____

**b**  didnt you know that sea slugs can regenerate parts of their body

_____

_____

**c**  delicious a sea slug thought the sea spider

_____

**Exploring Further ...**

Punctuation bingo!

With a friend, take turns to read sentences from a book. Cross out the punctuation on your board when you come across it!

Yours

| . | , | ? |
|---|---|---|
| ! | " " | ' |

_____'s

| . | , | ? |
|---|---|---|
| ! | " " | ' |

**Now ooze to pages 44–45 to record what you have learned in your explorer's logbook.**

# Picking possessives and plurals

**FACT FILE**

| | |
|---|---|
| **Animal:** | Starfish |
| **Habitat:** | All oceans of the world with the largest populations living in the Indian and Pacific Oceans |
| **Weight:** | From a few grams to 5 kg |
| **Lifespan:** | Up to 35 years |
| **Diet:** | Clams, shells and mussels |

There are two main uses for the **apostrophe.**

A **contraction**, when an apostrophe is used to show there is a letter(s) missing.

*don't* ⟶ *do not*      *we'll* ⟶ *we will*

The **possessive** apostrophe shows when something belongs to something else.

*The shell belonging to the crab* ⟶ *the crab's shell*

Adding **'s** to the end of a word turns it into a possessive plural.

*The fish of the children* ⟶ *the children's fish*

When a word already has a plural ending, the apostrophe goes at the end, and no further **s** is needed.

*The molluscs' shells* ⟶ *the shells of many molluscs*

---

**Task 1**    Read the following sentences. Underline the nouns and put a circle around the plurals.

**a** There are many species of starfish in the Pacific Ocean.

**b** Fishermen living in Bahamas' islands regularly catch cushion starfish.

**c** The pincushion starfish's body and arms are covered in tiny suckers.

**d** Starfish will run from the terrifying morning-sun starfish's many arms.

**Task 2**  Add apostrophes to the following phrases.

a  The childrens bucket.

b  The starfishs rock.

c  The giant clams pearl.

d  The Smiths fishing boat.

**WILD FACT**

Although they are named 'starfish', they are not related to fish at all. Starfish belong to the group: marine invertebrates.

**WILD FACT**

Most species of starfish have five arms, but there are sea stars with ten, twenty or even forty arms!

**Task 3**  Turn the phrases below into contracted phrases by using the possessive apostrophe.

a  The prey of the royal starfish is desperate to escape.

_____

b  The rock of the sunflower star is an important anchor point.

_____

c  The colouring of the necklace starfish makes it very attractive.

_____

d  The surface of the chocolate-chip sea star provides a home for tiny creatures.

_____

**Exploring Further ...**

Colour the arms on the starfish that contain possessive nouns.

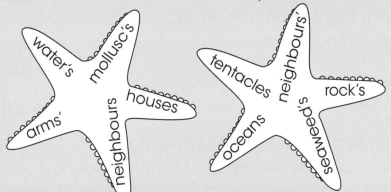

water's  mollusc's  houses  neighbours  arms'

tentacles  neighbours'  rock's  oceans  seaweed's

**Now twinkle to pages 44–45 to record what you have learned in your explorer's logbook.**

# Cracking conjunctions

## FACT FILE

**Animal:** Brittle star
**Habitat:** Oceans around the world, particularly the eastern Atlantic
**Weight:** Up to 5 kg
**Lifespan:** Around 10 years
**Diet:** Feeds on tiny particles found within sea water

When writing for an audience, it is important that we include all of the **detail** necessary as well as using varied vocabulary and smoothly flowing sentences, in a way that keeps the reader **interested**.

One simple way to improve the quality of your writing is to combine two short sentences into one longer, more interesting one. To do this we use **conjunctions**. These are words that join ideas within a sentence.

*but, yet, therefore, since, rather, than*

## Task 1

Complete the sentences by choosing the most appropriate conjunction from the brittle star's tentacles. Use each one only once.

**a** Its arms are covered in sharp spikes, _____ these are very fragile.

**b** The body of the brittle star is covered in spines _____ is roughly pentagonal in shape.

**c** The brittle star can be hard to spot _____ it is well camouflaged.

**d** It is also known as the 'serpent star' _____ its snake-like movements.

**e** Many other animals hunt the brittle star, _____ it spends much of its time hidden.

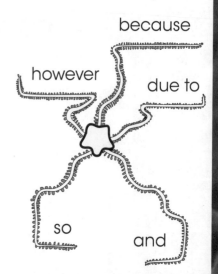

because
however
due to
so
and

24

**Task 2** Use three different colours to add full stops, capital letters and to circle any words that are spelt incorrectly.

brittle stars can be found in sees all over the world they have teeny bodies and five long arms with spiky bits on them brittle stars can break off these arms to escape meat-eating animals that hunt them the arms quickly grow back brittle stars can move fast in any direction usin there arms like legs to run on some people call them serpent stars coz they think they move like snakes they is hard to spot as they mainly come out at night

WILD FACT

They are also called 'serpent stars' because of the snakelike movements of their five slender arms.

**Task 3** Some of the vocabulary in the passage above could be improved. Look at the green words below and choose a word from the box to replace it.

| carnivorous | regenerate | small | predators | nocturnal |
| --- | --- | --- | --- | --- |

**a** teeny

**b** animals that hunt

**c** grow back

**d** meat-eating

**e** come out at night

### Exploring Further ...

Use your best handwriting to write out the paragraph from Task 2 again on a separate notepad or piece of paper, adding punctuation, correcting spelling mistakes and changing some of the words used to make it sound like a real biologist's report on the brittle star. Show your finished writing to someone to read and see how much you can teach them about this strange animal.

**Now feel your way to pages 44–45 to record what you have learned in your explorer's logbook.**

# What does it all mean?

## FACT FILE

**Animal:** Sand eel
**Habitat:** The coastlines of many European countries and America
**Weight:** 56 to 226 g
**Lifespan:** 3 to 10 years
**Diet:** Tiny fish, worms and plankton

As your reading develops, your **vocabulary** will also develop and, in turn, improve your writing. When you are learning to spell a new word, remember **LACAWAC** . . .

*Look and Cover and Write and Check!*

Top tip: Once you have learned to spell a new word, try to use it in a sentence as soon as possible. It will help you remember it.

## WILD FACT

Despite their name, sand eels are not true eels and are in fact fish.

---

**Task 1**  Draw six sand eels to match the words with their definitions.

| a definition | to get larger or bigger |
| b mention | to place or pull apart |
| c separate | what a word means |
| d increase | land surrounded by water |
| e decide | to say something in passing |
| f island | to make a choice |

## Task 2

How much would the words from Task 1 be worth in a game of Scrabble?

| A₁ | B₃ | C₃ | D₂ |
| E₁ | F₄ | G₂ | H₄ | I₁ | J₈ |
| K₅ | L₁ | M₃ | N₁ | O₁ | P₃ |
| Q₁₀ | R₁ | S₁ | T₁ | U₁ | V₄ |
| W₄ | X₈ | Y₄ | Z₁₀ |

a _____     b _____

c _____     d _____

e _____     f _____

## Task 3

Each word in the sand eel has been scrambled below. Work out which is which, and then write a definition for them.

medicine   library   special   address   height

**WILD FACT**

Female sand eels can produce between 4000 and 20 000 eggs in one spawn.

**a** laipecs _____

_____

**b** nimidece _____

_____

**c** lyrabir _____

_____

**d** thigeh _____

_____

**e** sedrasd _____

_____

### Exploring Further ...

Pick up the nearest book – the more random the better! – and choose five words from it that you don't know. Look them up in a dictionary, then use those words when speaking to someone within the next two hours. GO! The clock's started...!

**Now swim to pages 44–45 to record what you have learned in your explorer's logbook.**

# How do you know?

On these pages, you are going to improve your ability to **infer** and **deduce** about moods and feelings. In pictures, or with words, characters often reveal how they feel, even if they may not use the actual words to express how they are feeling.

*A character might not say, "I am feeling worried," but they may be described as fidgeting, or perhaps even stutter in speech. You can deduce their feelings by inferring how they are feeling from other clues, including body language and speech.*

## FACT FILE

**Animal:** Spider crab
**Habitat:** Throughout the world's oceans and seas
**Weight:** 2 to 19 kg
**Lifespan:** 5 to 100 years, depending on the species
**Diet:** Mainly seaweed and small fish

### Task 1

Draw lines to match the feeling word with the picture.

happy          surprised

upset          grumpy          worried

## WILD FACT

The Japanese spider crab has the largest leg-span of any arthropod in the world, reaching up to 3.8 metres from claw to claw!

**Task 2**

Read these extracts and write a couple of words to describe the character's mood. Underline any words or phrases that help you deduce the feeling.

a  "Ouch!" said the boy, shaking his hand forcefully in order to fling the crab from his finger.
What was he feeling? _____ _____

b  The children crept towards a rockpool and cautiously looked over the edge. The bottom wasn't visible from the surface. "Are you sure we need to find it?" asked the girl.
What was she feeling? _____ _____

c  The little boy raced across the beach, his bucket swinging wildly. Suddenly, he stopped and then poked a large pebble with his toe. "Got one, Dad!" he yelled.
What was he feeling? _____ _____

**Task 3**

Look at the comic strip below and describe how the characters are feeling.

I'm glad that question about spider crabs came up...

I can't believe I forgot to feed the shark!

WILD FACT

There are over 700 species of long, skinny-legged crabs throughout the world.

a _____   b _____

**Exploring Further ...**

Draw a character and write a speech bubble for it.
Can your friend guess the feeling of the character?

**Now skitter to pages 44–45 to record what you have learned in your explorer's logbook.**

# What happens next?

A fun thing to do when you are reading a book can be to stop halfway through a sentence and **think**, "I wonder what will come next?" Maybe you can **predict** what the character will do or how the story will end.

## FACT FILE

**Animal:** Puffin
**Habitat:** Coasts of Northern Europe, Greenland, Iceland, Canada and Alaska
**Weight:** Up to 500 g
**Lifespan:** Up to 25 years
**Diet:** Small fish, such as sand eels and herring

**Task 1** Look at how each of these facts start and draw a line to connect it to the correct ending.

The puffin's bright orange bill has led to it being nicknamed...

the 'sea parrot' and 'bottle nose'.

the 'monkey-sloths' and 'kangaroo-bear'.

Puffins can hold several small fish in their bills at a time because...

the insides of their mouth and tongue are rough and spiny.

they have three rows of sharp teeth capable of biting through bone.

Every year puffins go through their 'annual moult'. This is when...

they shed their skin and grow a whole new set of larger scales.

they shed their feathers and are unable to fly for a short while.

**Task 2**    Four of the sentences below are about puffins. Colour the sentences in.

| | |
|---|---|
| They make very good pets and can live in a bowl of cold water. | They are one of the most popular sea birds, known for being both colourful and full of character. |
| They are incredibly fast runners and can reach speeds of up to 81 kph (50 mph). | They are true seabirds and spend most of their time swimming, diving and feeding at sea. |
| The male is responsible for building the nest and the female lays only one egg in it. | Their sharp claws and strong arms make them expert tree climbers. |
| They kill their prey by tightly wrapping around it and suffocating it in a process called 'constriction'. | Thousands of them nest together in large groups called 'colonies'. |

**Task 3**    Using some of the facts found above, write a short story that tells us a little more about Percy the Puffin.

Percy Puffin lives in a burrow on a high cliff above the cold North Sea. With hundreds of his friends and family, Percy loves to _____

_____

_____

_____

**WILD FACT**

Puffins are excellent fliers. Flapping their wings at up to 400 beats per minute, they can reach speeds of 88 km/h (55 mph).

**Exploring Further ...**

Try to match the animal below to their nickname. Draw a line of puffin prints to match them up!

| | |
|---|---|
| koalas | egg-suckers |
| butterflies | hotchi-witchi |
| toucans | monkey-bears |
| hedgehogs | sneak-cats |
| pumas | bobby-dazzler |

**Now burrow to pages 44–45 to record what you have learned in your explorer's logbook.**

# Understanding what we read

One of the best things about **reading** is that it gives you the ability to **discover** endless **exciting facts** about the world around you. Experts researching animals will often go back to the books **written by others** before them to help them better understand the animals that really interest them. On these pages we will use our **comprehension** skills to find out all about the rather odd-looking lumpfish!

## WILD FACT

People like to eat the small eggs laid by the lumpfish. They are famous for their salty taste and the way they 'pop' on the tongue.

## FACT FILE

**Animal:** Lumpfish
**Habitat:** Cold waters of the Arctic, North Pacific and North Atlantic
**Weight:** Up to 9 kg
**Lifespan:** 5 to 15 years
**Diet:** Small sealife, including shrimp

### Task 1

Below is the contents page from a non-fiction book about lumpfish. Which page would you turn to if you wanted to know...

**a** ... how to identify a lumpfish?

**b** ... what a word in the book means?

**c** ... where to find a lumpfish?

**d** ... if lumpfish are carnivores or not?

**e** ... how long a lumpfish lives?

**Contents**

**Task 2**

Below are some words and four definitions from the glossary of a book. Draw a line to join the correct word to the definition.

**WILD FACT**

Lumpfish get their name from the lumpy, wart-like growths that cover their thick skin.

 carnivore

 North Atlantic

 roe

 pectoral fins

A mass of eggs released by female fish.

The world's second largest ocean, between Europe and Africa to the east, and the Americas to the west.

The pair of fins found either side of a fish's head, used to control movement.

An animal that feeds on the flesh of other animals as the key part of its diet.

**Task 3**

Read the non-fiction text below and then write three questions that you think someone should be able to answer.

The lumpfish is known by some as the 'lumpsucker.' It has a short, fat body. It does not have scales but rather thick, lumpy skin. Large lumpfish can reach up to 60 cm in length and 5 to 6 kg in weight. They are found within cold northern waters, such as the North Atlantic. The lumpfish is a carnivore, eating a diet of smaller fish and tiny sea creatures.

1 _____

2 _____

3 _____

**Exploring Further ...**

Show the text extract in Task 3 to a friend or family member and ask them your questions. See how well they answer, giving marks out of 3!

1: Lumpfish brain!                    2: Getting saltier . . .

3: Fish and chips for tea!

**Now swim to pages 44–45 to record what you have learned in your explorer's logbook.**

# Summarising reports

Writing a **summary** for a piece of text means you need to write a list of the **main points**. It can help to underline the key points in the writing. Key features of a summary:
- *List form*
- *Chronological order*
- *Keep only the main facts*
- *Remove most descriptive language*

**FACT FILE**

| | |
|---|---|
| **Animal:** | Pseudoscorpion |
| **Habitat:** | From cold regions of the United States to tropical regions along the equator |
| **Weight:** | A few grams |
| **Lifespan:** | 2 to 3 years |
| **Diet:** | Ants, mites and small flies |

**Task 1** Use the information below to write a paragraph about the pseudoscorpion's habitat. Make sure you write in sentences.

- Different species live in woodland, seashores, rocks and grassland.
- Often found in homes and beneficial to humans, as they eat dust mites and tiny flies.
- Live in 'clumps' (groups), which are larger in tropical areas.
- They can travel longer distances by hitching a ride on larger insects, such as flies and beetles.

_____

_____

_____

_____

_____

**Task 2**

Using the fact file and the report below, summarise the **lifecycle** of the pseudoscorpion.

**WILD FACT**

Pseudoscorpions (also known as 'false scorpions') are not actually scorpions at all but a type of arachnid, meaning they belong to the same class of animals as spiders.

Pseudo means 'pretend', and this scorpion is more like a spider. It has eight legs a flat, pear-shaped body and a pair of pincers. Its abdomen is short and rounded in shape and does not end with a sting. They catch their prey in a pincer, poison it with venom from a venom duct and then eat the liquid remains from the prey. Gloopy!

The pseudoscorpion spins a silk cocoon in which it lays fertilised eggs. After hatching, the young then spend some time riding on the mother, for safety. As the young grow, they moult their skin and may moult as many as three times before adulthood.

Tropical areas of the world have the most dense populations of pseudoscorpions, and they can often be found in homes. They can actually be helpful to humans as they eat the larvae of flies, ants and mites.

_____

_____

_____

_____

**WILD FACT**

Pseudoscorpions look exactly like scorpions but without the stinging tail.

**Exploring Further …**

How many words can you make from 'Pseudoscorpion'? You may use each letter only once. Award yourself one point for each letter used. Ask a friend to play. Who has the better score?

_____

_____

_____

**Now scuttle to pages 44–45 to record what you have learned in your explorer's logbook.**

# Hold the headline!

**FACT FILE**

**Animal:** Prawn
**Habitat:** Waters throughout the world
**Weight:** 20 to 50 g
**Lifespan:** 1 to 4 years
**Diet:** Small fish, insects and plankton

**Headlines** are the big words at the top of **newspaper** articles. **Tabloid** papers are smaller-sized newspapers that often carry news about celebrities, or 'shocking' stories. **Broadsheet** newspapers are larger and have articles about politics and the economy.

Headlines are used to catch people's attention, using the following **tricks of the trade**:

- Alliteration: using words starting with the same letters

  **PINK PRAWNS PRODUCE PUTRID PONG!**

- Rhyme

  **FAT CAT MISTAKEN FOR HAT**

- Changing a letter to give the word a double meaning.

  **BALDNESS: 'HAIR' TODAY GONE TOMORROW**

- Puns: using a word that can have two meanings.

  **BAKER LOSES A BUN-DLE**

---

**Task 1**    Match the start of the newspaper article to the headline.

**a** A record catch of prawns was hauled up by the trawler the *Marie Rose*.

**What the blazes?**

**b** Factory workers were amazed when frozen prawns came back to life after defrosting.

**Prawn cocktail Marie**

**c** A fire at a prawn factory late last night took five fire engines to bring it under control.

**Prawn of the Dead**

**Task 2**   Are these headlines from a broadsheet newspaper or a tabloid newspaper?

a **Fish and Tips** – Chip shop waitress' story

_____

b **Limited stocks see prices soar** – Fewer prawns in the ocean _____

c **Cod you win first plaice?** – Competition to win aquarium passes

_____

**WILD FACT**

Prawns have five pairs of legs: the rear three pairs are used for walking, while the front two pairs are used for eating.

**Task 3**   Make up a punchy headline for the stories below.

a A boat was caught in a storm. A crew member fell overboard, but they were rescued. (Broadsheet)

_____

b A group of tourists got cut off by the rising tide and were rescued by helicopter. (Tabloid)

_____

c Last year's _Mastercook_ winner cooked for the Prime Minister. He was delighted. (Tabloid)

_____

**WILD FACT**

Prawns have very long antenna that can sense any danger close by and are also used to detect food.

**Exploring Further ...**

Can you write a 'story in a nutshell' for this headline?

**Grandma has shocking sushi!**

_____

_____

_____

**Now drift to pages 44–45 to record what you have learned in your explorer's logbook.**

# Dear diary

A diary is usually written in the **first person**, using '**I**' or '**me**'. It is written in **chronological** order, with the earliest event first. It is about events that have already happened, so is written in the **past tense**. There should be '**time**' words at the start of some sentences. It will usually contain the thoughts and feelings of the writer.

*Today I got up early and went into town. After lunch, we went to the cinema. The film was ace! It was better than the first one, and I loved it!*

**FACT FILE**

| | |
|---|---|
| **Animal:** | Sea otter |
| **Habitat:** | The shallow waters of the Pacific Ocean |
| **Weight:** | 14 to 45 kg |
| **Lifespan:** | Up to 23 years |
| **Diet:** | Fish and sea urchins |

**Task 1**  Read these imaginary diary extracts written by a sea otter mum.  Put the events in chronological order by writing numbers 1–5 in the box next to each extract.

**a**  Today, I taught my cub how to swim. She is really starting to get the hang of using her tail to move through the water.

**b**  This afternoon was incredible. My beautiful cub arrived safely into the world. She was born in the water and had her eyes wide open.

**c**  My cub is growing bigger. Soon she'll stop drinking my milk, and she'll be ready to eat some fish.

**d**  My clever girl was able to dive down to get a shell from the sea bed today!  I am so proud of her.

**e**  My tiny cub can't swim far yet, so she usually spends her day on my tummy.

38

**Task 2** In 1989, there was a huge oil spill from a cargo ship called the *Exxon Valdez*. Read each diary extract carefully and draw a line to its correct date.

| | |
|---|---|
| 24 March 2001 | The fish population has been badly affected, with a loss of $31 million to the fishing industry. |
| 24 March 1989 | So far, as many as 2800 sea otters have died, and other sea birds and animals have died too. |
| 2 April 1991 | Even 12 years later, oil traces can be found on over half the beaches that were affected. |
| 30 March 1989 | The oil tanker, the *Exxon Valdez*, spilled 10.8 million gallons of oil into the sea. |

**Task 3** Add some ideas and details to this diary.

**WILD FACT**

Sea otters have been known to cover themselves in kelp seaweed to stop themselves from drifting away!

Day 1: I saw the sea otters today. I was excited because _____

_____.

Day 3: One of the younger sea otters was _____

I felt _____.

Day 4: It looked like the otters were having a diving competition

off the rocks. They were _____

which made me feel _____.

Day 6: One of the otters was cracking open a shell on the rock

today. They seem to eat a lot! I wonder _____

_____.

**Exploring Further ...**

Write a diary entry about a time you have watched wildlife. Use the past tense; start with 'I'; include your thoughts and feelings.

_____

_____

_____

_____

**Now dive to pages 44–45 to record what you have learned in your explorer's logbook.**

39

# Perfecting your poetry

**Poetry** is a type of writing that has been around for hundreds of years. The idea of a poem is that it gives the author the chance to **express ideas** or **feelings** in a relatively short piece of writing that will interest and entertain the reader.

Many people think that poems have to include rhyming words . . .

*'bird' and 'heard'*      *'sky' and 'pie'*      *'write' and 'bright'*

or to give the poem a rhythm or pattern when read aloud. This isn't actually true: poems can do anything!

---

| Task 1 | For words to rhyme, they must make the same sound when read aloud. Try these – the first one has been done for you. |
|---|---|

**a** gull      rhymes with      *hull*

**b** black      rhymes with      _____

**c** fly      rhymes with      _____

**d** flock      rhymes with      _____

**e** fish      rhymes with      _____

**f** eggs      rhymes with      _____

## FACT FILE

**Animal:** Black-headed gull
**Habitat:** Europe, Asia and Canada
**Weight:** 200 to 400 g
**Lifespan:** They often live a long life, with a maximum recorded lifespan of 32 years!
**Diet:** Worms, insects and fish

## WILD FACT

These gulls often live in large, noisy groups that can upset their human neighbours.

**Task 2**  Now put each pair of rhyming words into a sentence. The first one is done for you.

**a** The tired gull landed on the ship's hull.

**b** _____.

**c** _____.

**d** _____.

**e** _____.

**f** _____.

**Task 3**  Poems are often meant to be told by someone who knows the poem 'off by heart'. Read this poem, then close the page and see if you can still remember it.

### The Little Bird

Once I saw a little bird,

Come hop, hop, hop;

So I cried, little bird,

Will you stop, stop, stop?

And was going to the window,

To say how do you do?

But he shook his little tail,

And far away he flew.

**WILD FACT**

During summer, the feathers on the gull's head turn a chocolate-brown colour, rather than black.

**Exploring Further ...**

Now you know the poem of *The Little Bird*, practise reciting it out loud, adding expression and ensuring that you add the pauses and breaths where the punctuation shows they should be. When you think you are ready for an audience, try reciting the poem to a friend or your family!

**Now swoop to pages 44–45 to record what you have learned in your explorer's logbook.**

# Quick test

Now try these questions. Give yourself 1 mark for every correct answer – but only if you answer each part of the question correctly!

1 **Circle the disyllabic words.**

exercise    rockpool    jellyfish    beach    ocean

2 **Colour the boxes that contain correctly spelt words.**

| diferent | British | different | Brittish |

3 **Write the homophones that mean 'opposite of day' and 'historical man wearing armour'.**

_____ and _____

4 **Circle the correct spelling of the word that means an 'exciting or unusual experience'.**

advensure    advencher    adventure

5 **Add a prefix to these words to make them negative.**

_____ legal        _____ mature

6 **Write the root word of 'various'.** _____

7 **Say these words out loud. One phoneme sounds different. Circle the odd word out.**

eight    reign    height    neighbour

8 **Write the following words in your best handwriting, using joined letters: perfect pelican**

_____

9 **Choose the end of the sentence that makes sense. Tick one.**
The library has a…

- special books section. ☐
- carpet workshop area. ☐
- permanent rock collection. ☐

10 **Write a word that means '100 years'.** _____

11 **Read the extract and underline the words that show the character is feeling worried:**

The boy looked at the huge number of crabs scrambling over each other in the tank. His eyes widened and his lips trembled, and he backed away quickly, as it looked as though they could spill over the top."

12 **Read the following extract and write two points to summarise the report:**

"The albatross is a truly amazing bird, spending most of its life in flight. It uses a technique called dynamic soaring to catch the updraft of wind currents and can spend up to seven years in continuous flight."

_____

_____

**13 Choose the headline to suit this story:**

Surprised granny, Edna, was enjoying her fish and chips on the beach when a starfish landed in her lap. She purchased a lottery ticket later that day, but we await to find out the results of the draw.

| Pensioner lands a starfish | Star-struck lady may be lucky | Lottery win for starfish lady |
| --- | --- | --- |

**14 Put these diary events in order by numbering them.**

| Brought home the fish for the aquarium. It's great to see them darting around. | I can't believe it's Mabel's first birthday! Bought special fish flakes. | Bought my first aquarium today! I put stones and weeds in the bottom. |
| --- | --- | --- |

**15 Rewrite these sentences to include the extra phrase, to make them more interesting.**

The jellyfish moves through the water.          by slowly pulsating

_____

The crab scuttles under a rock.          huge grey

_____

**16 Underline the part of the following extract that answers the question.**

Q: What do all seashore animals have in common?

By definition, the seashore is really any place where the land meets the sea. It is home to a truly diverse range of creatures, which are fascinating to study, One quality of these animals is that they must be able to adapt and develop in order to withstand a difficult and constantly changing environment.

**17 Can you recite the poem that starts "Once I saw a little bird..." from page 41?**

**18 Mark the true statements with a tick and the false statements with a cross.**

. Starfish live in a colony. ☐          . Starfish only have five arms. ☐

. Starfishes' arms have small suckers. ☐          . Some starfish eat each other! ☐

**19 Add punctuation to the following sentence:**

when you visit the seaside treat any animals you find with respect make a note of the tide changes and stay away from rocky cliffs follow the seashore code

**20 Add words from the box below to make the sentence more interesting.**

| rich | fascinating | curious |
| --- | --- | --- |

The seashore makes an exciting and _____ environment for those looking

to uncover the secrets of some of the _____ and _____

wildlife living there.

How did you do?   **1–5 Try again!**   **6–10 Good try!**   **/20**

**11–15 Great work!**   **16–20 Excellent exploring!**

# Explorer's Logbook

Tick off the topics as you complete them and then colour in the star.

How do you feel?
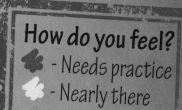
- Needs practice
- Nearly there
- Got it!

Delivering details ☐

Slippery spellings ☐

Superb suffixes ☐

Super syllables ☐

Helping with handwriting ☐

Handling homophones ☐

Practising prefixes ☐

Sorting out syllables ☐

Figuring out phonemes ☐

Summarising reports ☐

What does it all mean? ☐

Putting in punctuation ☐

How do you know? ☐

Perfecting your poetry ☐

Understanding what we read ☐

Picking possessives and plurals ☐

Cracking conjunctions ☐

Dear diary ☐

What happens next? ☐

Hold the headline! ☐

# Answers

## Pages 2–3

### Task 1
Lines should be traced carefully following the pattern in a continuous line from left to right.

### Task 2
Letters should look like the demonstration letters, and be of a consistent size and height.

### Task 3
Letters should sit on the line and hang below it. The letters should be of a consistent size.

### Exploring Further...
A neatly written sentence with even height letters.

## Pages 4–5

### Task 1
| | | | |
|---|---|---|---|
| a | 1 | b | 3 |
| c | 2 | d | 2 |
| e | 4 | f | 2 |
| g | 1 | h | 3 |
| i | 2 | j | 5 |

### Task 2
| | | | |
|---|---|---|---|
| a | pi-a-no | b | his-tory |
| c | cal-en-dar | d | ex-per-i-ment |

### Task 3
| | | | |
|---|---|---|---|
| a | heart | b | famous |
| c | busy | d | remember |

### Exploring Further...

| monosyllabic words | disyllabic words | Polysyllabic words |
|---|---|---|
| shark | turtle | camera |
| | seaweed | jellyfish |
| | dolphin | crocodile (or 'alligator') |

## Pages 6–7

### Task 1
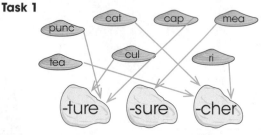

### Task 2
| Disyllabic words | Trisyllabic words | Polysyllabic words |
|---|---|---|
| treasure | adventure | agriculture |
| future | miniature | |
| leisure | furniture | |
| nature | enclosure | |
| preacher | | |

### Task 3
| | | | |
|---|---|---|---|
| a | fracture | b | pasture |
| c | stretcher | d | temperature |

### Exploring Further...
For example: The rancher went on a furniture adventure to find treasure.

## Pages 8–9

### Task 1
| | | | | | |
|---|---|---|---|---|---|
| a | different | b | appear | c | breathe |

### Task 2
Circled: strainge, throogh, diffecult, arive, suprise

## Task 3
| | | | |
|---|---|---|---|
| 1 | strange | 2 | through |
| 3 | difficult | 4 | arrive |
| 5 | surprise | | |

### Exploring Further...
Man o' war, Cross, Box, Lion's Mane.

## Pages 10–11

### Task 1
| fair | → | fare | knew | → | new |
|---|---|---|---|---|---|
| write | → | right | here | → | hear |
| no | → | know | knight | → | night |

### Task 2
This doughnut has a **hole** in the middle.
I can eat a **whole** doughnut in one bite.
It gets dark at **night**.
The **knight** rides on a white horse.

### Task 3
grown — To have become ...
toe — To pull ...
cell — A very small ...
groan — A deep sound ...
tow — To exchange...
sell — Our feet ...

### Exploring Further...
No answer required.

## Pages 12–13

### Task 1
| | | | | | |
|---|---|---|---|---|---|
| a | catch | b | climb | c | knit |
| d | wrong | e | near | f | pinch |
| g | chemist | h | phone | i | knowledge |
| j | ledge | | | | |

### Task 2
| fr**oo**t | fruit | w**ate** | wait |
|---|---|---|---|
| g**ide** | guide | wr**oa**t | wrote |
| br**yt** | bright | compl**eat** | complete |
| gr**oop** | group | bri**ethe** | breathe |
| b**ede** | bead | extr**eam** | extreme |

### Task 3
| | | | | | |
|---|---|---|---|---|---|
| a | s**ch**ool | b | h**eight** | c | peng**ui**n |
| d | sw**a**llow | e | s**ea** | | |

### Exploring Further...

|   |   |   |   |   |   |   |   |
|---|---|---|---|---|---|---|---|
| ¹r | e | e | ³f | | | | |
| | | | i | | | | |
| ⁴j | e | l | l | y | f | i | ²s | h |
| | | | t | | | | q |
| | | ⁵y | e | a | r | | u |
| | | | r | | | | i |
| | | | | ⁶w | o | r | l | d |
| | | | | | | | t |

## Pages 14–15

### Task 1
| in- | im- | ir- | il- |
|---|---|---|---|
| indescribable | immature | irreplaceable | illicit |
| informer | impersonal | irregular | illuminate |
| | improbable | irrational | |

## Task 2

Use **il** for words that begin with 'l'.
Use **ir** for words that begin with 'r'.
Use **im** for words that begin with 'm' or 'p'.
Use **in** for words that begin with all other letters.

### Task 3

| Root word | Add correct prefix |
|---|---|
| correct, visible, formal, expensive | in |
| possible | im |
| responsible | ir |
| legal | il |

### Exploring Further...

| in | active | im | legible | in | correct |
|---|---|---|---|---|---|
| il | migrant | possible | ir | polite | il |
| formal | in | il | legal | im | right |
| ir | im | expensive | ir | luminate | in |
| patient | correct | im | regular | il | relevant |
| responsible | il | in | patient | former | im |

## Pages 16–17
### Task 1

a melodious    b adventurous
c dangerous    d glorious
e courageous    f furious

### Task 2

a dangerous      b poisonous
c nervous      d mountainous
e various

### Task 3

Remove the last two letters and add the **ous** suffix.

### Exploring Further...

Ravenous, industrious, adventurous.
'Urchinous' is not a real word.

## Pages 18–19
### Task 1

crawl   swim   sleep   swoop

~~deadly~~
~~poisonous~~
~~smooth~~
~~patterned~~

### Task 2

Gently,      I go swimming.
Suddenly,      he leapt forward.
On holiday,      I love to read.
Once a week,      he lifted up the baby.

### Task 3

For example: The deadly tarantula is highly poisonous etc.

### Exploring Further...

For example: Unexpectedly, the small, spotty dogfish charged out from behind the large limpet-covered rock where it had been hiding to avoid the child's net.

## Pages 20–21
### Task 1

a It's amazing how much a sea slug eats!
b Do sea slugs live on coral?
c There are over 1000 species of sea slug!
d How does a sea slug eat?
e How many species of sea slug are there?

### Task 2

(It's), don't, they're, can't, aren't, I've

## Task 3

a More than 1000 species of sea slug live on Australia's Great Barrier Reef.
b Didn't you know that sea slugs can regenerate parts of their body?
c "Delicious! A sea slug," thought the sea spider.

### Exploring Further...

Did you win?

## Pages 22–23
### Task 1

a There are many species of starfish in the Pacific Ocean.
b Fishermen living in Bahamas' islands regularly catch cushion starfish.
c The pincushion starfish's body and arms are covered in tiny suckers.
d Starfish will run from the terrifying morning-sun starfish's many arms.

### Task 2

a children's      b starfish's
c clam's      d Smiths'

### Task 3

a The royal starfish's prey ...
b The sunflower star's rock ...
c The necklace starfish's colouring ...
d The chocolate-chip sea star's surface ...

### Exploring Further...

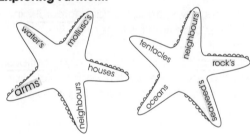

## Pages 24–25
### Task 1

a however      b and      c because
d due to      e so

### Task 2

**Brittle stars can be found in sees all over the world. They have teeny bodies and five long arms with spiky bits on them. Brittle stars can break off these arms to escape meat-eating animals that hunt them. The arms quickly grow back. Brittle stars can move fast in any direction usin there arms like legs to run on. Some people call them serpent stars coz they think they move like snakes. They is hard to spot as they mainly come out at night.**

### Task 3

a teeny – small
b animals that hunt – predators
c grow back – regenerate
d meat-eating – carnivores
e come out at night – nocturnal

### Exploring Further...

Writing to link ideas in a sensible, free-flowing way, with correct spellings and sentences correctly punctuated.

## Pages 26–27

### Task 1

a  definition — what a word means
b  mention — to say something in passing
c  separate — to place or pull apart
d  increase — to get larger or bigger
e  decide — to make a choice
f  island — land surrounded by water

### Task 2

a  definition = 14
b  mention = 9
c  separate = 10
d  increase = 10
e  decide = 10
f  island = 7

### Task 3

a  special: better, greater or different from the usual
b  medicine: liquid or pill given to make ill people better
c  library: a room with books that can be borrowed
d  height: how tall an object or person is
e  address: information needed to say how to find a particular building. Written on letters and parcels.

## Pages 28–29

### Task 1

upset   surprised   happy   worried   grumpy

### Task 2

a  "Ouch!" said the boy, shaking his hand <u>forcefully</u>, in order to fling the crab from his finger.
Shocked, angry
b  The children <u>crept</u> towards a rockpool and <u>cautiously</u> looked over the edge. The bottom wasn't visible from the surface. "Are you sure we need to find it?" asked the girl. Worried, anxious or nervous
c  The little boy <u>raced</u> across the beach, his bucket swinging wildly, Suddenly, he stopped, and then poked a large pebble with his toe. <u>"Got one, Dad!" he yelled.</u> Excited, delighted

### Task 3

a  The woman is pleased, relieved.
b  The woman is worried, alarmed or upset.

### Exploring Further...

Your own picture with a speech bubble.

## Pages 30–31

### Task 1

a  The puffin's bright ⟶ 'the sea parrot'
b  Puffins can hold ⟶ the insides of their mouth
c  Every year puffins ⟶ they shed their feathers

### Task 2

| | |
|---|---|
| Thousands of them nest together in large groups called 'colonies'. | They are one of the most popular sea birds, known for being both colourful and full of character. |
| The male is responsible for building the nest and the female lays only one egg in it. | They are true seabirds and spend most of their time swimming, diving and feeding at sea. |

### Task 3

Any correctly spelt story.

## Exploring Further...

egg-suckers — hedgehogs
hotchi-witchi — koalas
monkey-bears — toucans
sneak-cats — butterflies
bobby-dazzler — pumas

## Pages 32–33

### Task 1

a  Page 25
b  Page 103
c  Page 1
d  Page 57
e  Page 93

### Task 2

carnivore An animal that feeds ...
North Atlantic The world's second ...
roe A mass of eggs ...
pectoral fins The pair of fins ...

### Task 3

For example:
By what name is the lumpfish also known as?
The lumpfish is not covered in scales. What is it covered in?
Which ocean are lumpfish found in?
How big are fully grown lumpfish?
What do lumpfish eat?

### Exploring Further...

Ask your family or a friend the questions in task 3.

## Pages 34–35

### Task 1

Paragraph should make sense and be written in complete sentences. Words and phrases from the points should be included.

### Task 2

Ensure the points cover <u>only</u> the lifecycle of the pseudoscorpion, as this was what the question asked for.

### Exploring Further...

For example: scorpion, does, cross, pious, drip, croon, door, pour, nips, poison, spins

## Pages 36–37

### Task 1

a  Prawn cocktail Marie
b  Prawn of the Dead
c  What the blazes?

### Task 2

a  Tabloid
b  Broadsheet
c  Tabloid

### Task 3

For example:
a  Man in deep water now safe
b  Dramatic rescue for tourists
c  Exquisite eats for PM

### Exploring Further...

Any story involving a grandmother, sushi and a shock!

## Pages 38–39

### Task 1

a 4, b 1, c 3, d 5, e 2

### Task 2

| 24 March 1989 | The oil tanker, the *Exxon Valdez*, spilled 10.8 million gallons of oil into the sea. |
|---|---|
| 30 March 1989 | So far, as many as 2800 sea otters have died, and other sea birds and animals have died too. |